ESSENTIAL L-TEST TECHNIQUES
—In Pictures

ESSENTIAL
L - TEST
TECHNIQUES
—In Pictures

Brian Phillips DOE, ADI, MIAM

Foulis

Haynes

ISBN 0 85429 465 1

© B.J. Phillips 1985
First published 1985

A FOULIS Motoring Book

Published by:
Haynes Publishing Group
Sparkford, Yeovil, Somerset BA22 7JJ

Haynes Publications Inc.
861 Lawrence Drive, Newbury Park, California 91320 USA

British Library Cataloguing in Publication Data

Phillips, Brian J.
    L - test techniques : in pictures.
    1. Automobile driving
    I. Title
    629.28'32   TL152.5
    ISBN 0–85429–465–1

Editor: Mansur Darlington
Page layout: Graham Thompson
Jacket illustration: Doug Kenyon
Printed and bound by: J.H. Haynes & Co Ltd

CONTENTS

Page

INTRODUCTION

Learning to drive is probably one of the most exciting times of your life and as the first driving lesson draws nearer, a slight feeling of apprehension begins to creep in.

Whether you intend to have a relative or friend teach you, or to take lessons with a professional driving instructor, you will be assisted in the learning process if you have a book to help you.

L-Test Techniques in Pictures has been produced because to many learners a good clear diagram of a particular manoeuvre is more helpful than a page of print. In it will be found over 30 diagrams which are clearly laid out and easy to follow by the beginner, and which show many of the basic manoeuvres that the learner will be required to master.

This excellent booklet, used in conjunction with your *Highway Code*, will help you considerably to adopt a clean-cut system for everything you do whilst behind the wheel.

The book is not intended to be a complete guide to learning to drive but simply to clarify some of the manoeuvres and systems required leading up to your test; procedures, it is hoped, that will remain with you throughout your driving career.

The booklet DL68 *Your Driving Test* goes into detail on the requirements of the test and so they are not covered in any great depth here.

Study your diagrams and practise each one thoroughly until it simply 'flows', and with lots of practice and some expert guidance it will not be too long before you are ready to pass your driving test.

The advice given in this book is based upon the practical experience, gained over many years, of a highly qualified driving instructor. It should be noted, however, that much of driving practice is a matter of opinion and interpretation. In view of this, neither the author nor the publishers can accept liability for any damage, loss or injury caused as a result of errors or omissions in the information given.

10 GENERAL HINTS CONCERNING YOUR DRIVING

1   Do not cross your arms except when manoeuvring in a confined space. This is very unlikely to occur during the test.

2   Observe all speed limits at all times.

3   All diagrams in this booklet show braking as the means of reducing your speed. On slippery roads it is often safer to change down through the gears in addition to using the brakes so as to prevent any possibility of skidding. In extreme weather conditions, such as ice or snow, allow much more distance for reducing speed and, in some cases use the gearbox only, avoiding the use of the brakes altogether.

4   Do not follow too closely to the vehicle in front. Leave a gap of at least 1 metre for each mph, and double this, at least, when the roads are wet.

5   When driving down steep hills use a lower gear to avoid prolonged use of the brakes which may cause overheating of the brake drums or discs. A good guideline is to use the same gear going down as you would need to come up.

6   On the open road use your brakes to reduce your speed on the approach to bends and not whilst driving around them because this may cause your wheels to lock especially if the road is slippery or wet. Use gentle acceleration when coming out of the bend.

7   Good lane discipline is very important, especially in busy towns, so plan well ahead and make sure you get in the correct lane early.

8   Always be in the correct position, driving at the correct speed, and in the correct gear for the road you are on.

9   Never drive at a speed whereby you cannot pull up well within the distance seen to be clear.

10 If you are learning to drive in a vehicle with an automatic gearbox make sure you understand the correct way to use the selector; this should be explained clearly in the handbook or manual. This type of vehicle has certain characteristics about its handling and driving technique which have to be carefully mastered.

COCKPIT DRILL

When entering your vehicle always check in the following order that:-

1   Your door is properly closed by pushing once after shutting.
2   The handbrake is on.
3   The gear lever is in neutral by moving side to side.
4   Your seat is correctly positioned for you.
5   Your mirrors are correctly adjusted.
6   You put your seat belt on before driving off.

....

The examiner will note whether or not this drill is carried out at the beginning of your test.

SPEEDS THROUGH THE GEARS

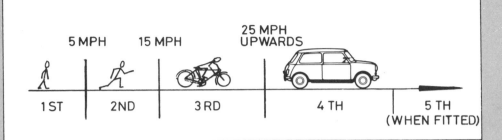

5 MPH   15 MPH   25 MPH
                              UPWARDS

1 ST   2 ND   3 RD   4 TH   5 TH
                                                    (WHEN FITTED)

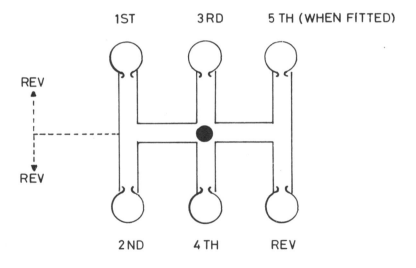

1ST   3RD   5 TH (WHEN FITTED)

REV
REV

2 ND   4 TH   REV

APPROXIMATE SPEED RANGES IN EACH GEAR FOR
AN AVERAGE FAMILY CAR

STEERING TECHNIQUE (LEFT-HAND TURN)

'NORMAL DRIVING' POSITION FOR THE HANDS		BETWEEN QUARTER TO THREE AND TEN TO TWO POSITION
LEFT HAND TO TOP		RIGHT HAND STAYS STILL
LEFT HAND PULLS WHEEL DOWN		RIGHT HAND SLIDES DOWN
LEFT HAND SLIDES UP		RIGHT HAND PUSHES WHEEL UP
LEFT HAND PULLS WHEEL DOWN		RIGHT HAND SLIDES DOWN
LEFT HAND SLIDES UP		RIGHT HAND PUSHES WHEEL UP

NOTE: TO TURN RIGHT MERELY REVERSE THE PROCEDURE

WHY YOU NEED TO LOOK RIGHT & LEFT IN ADDITION TO USING YOUR MIRRORS

H8716

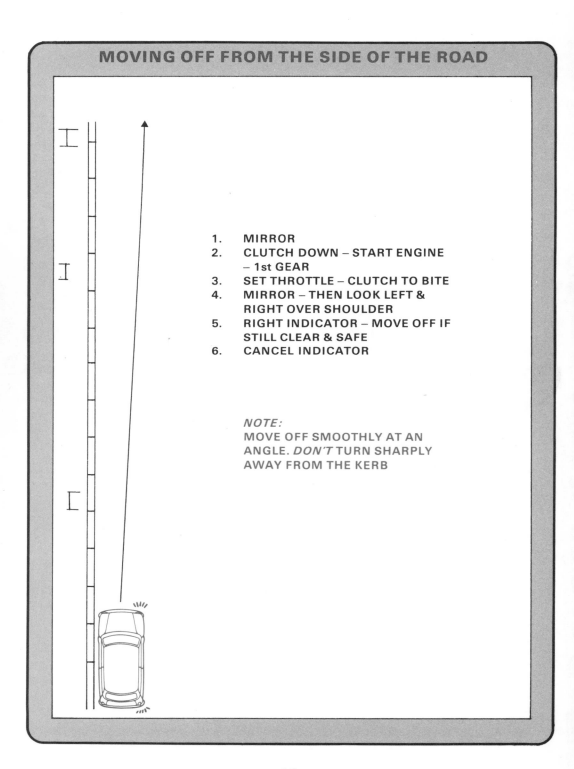

MOVING OFF FROM THE SIDE OF THE ROAD

1. MIRROR
2. CLUTCH DOWN – START ENGINE
   – 1st GEAR
3. SET THROTTLE – CLUTCH TO BITE
4. MIRROR – THEN LOOK LEFT &
   RIGHT OVER SHOULDER
5. RIGHT INDICATOR – MOVE OFF IF
   STILL CLEAR & SAFE
6. CANCEL INDICATOR

NOTE:
MOVE OFF SMOOTHLY AT AN
ANGLE. *DON'T* TURN SHARPLY
AWAY FROM THE KERB

1. MIRROR
2. LEFT INDICATOR
3. MOVE TOWARDS KERB
4. BRAKE TO STOP
5. APPLY HANDBRAKE
6. GEAR LEVER TO NEUTRAL
7. CANCEL INDICATOR

NOTE:
HANDBRAKE ON *BEFORE* NEUTRAL

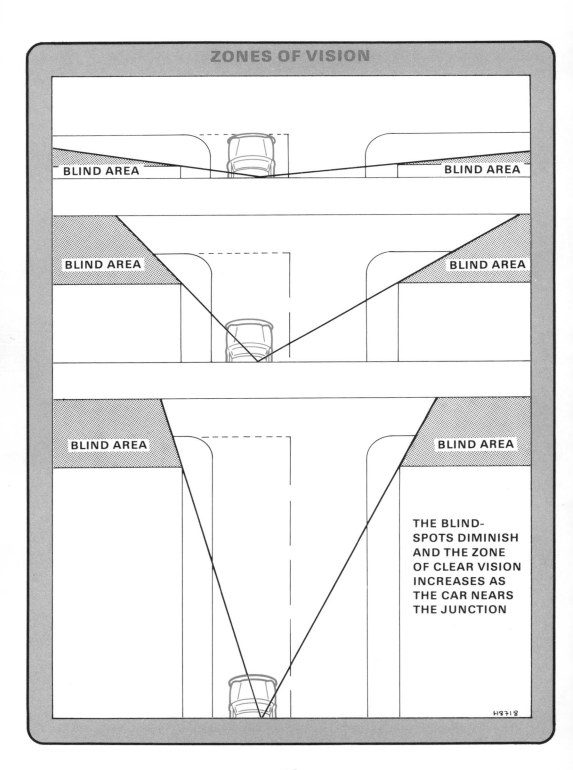

ZONES OF VISION

BLIND AREA

BLIND AREA

BLIND AREA

BLIND AREA

BLIND AREA

BLIND AREA

THE BLIND-
SPOTS DIMINISH
AND THE ZONE
OF CLEAR VISION
INCREASES AS
THE CAR NEARS
THE JUNCTION

H8718

PROCEDURE AT 'GIVE-WAY' JUNCTIONS

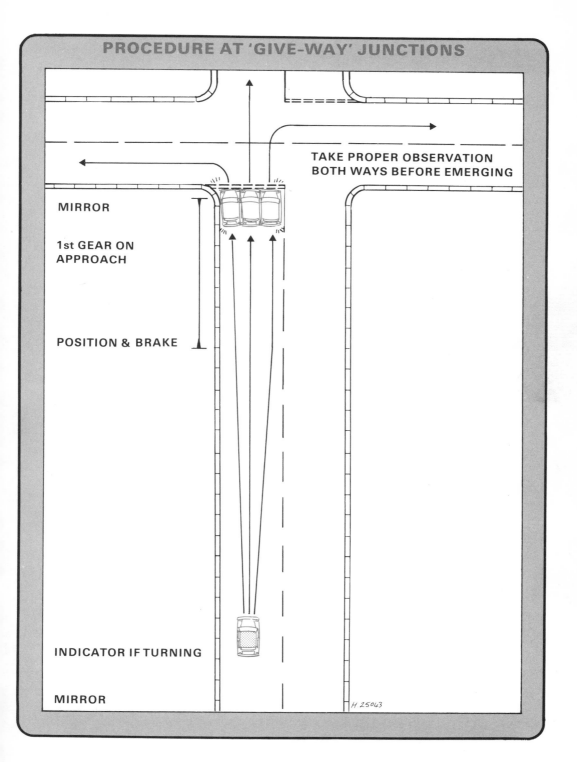

TAKE PROPER OBSERVATION
BOTH WAYS BEFORE EMERGING

MIRROR

1st GEAR ON
APPROACH

POSITION & BRAKE

INDICATOR IF TURNING

MIRROR

H 25043

PROCEDURE AT 'STOP' JUNCTIONS

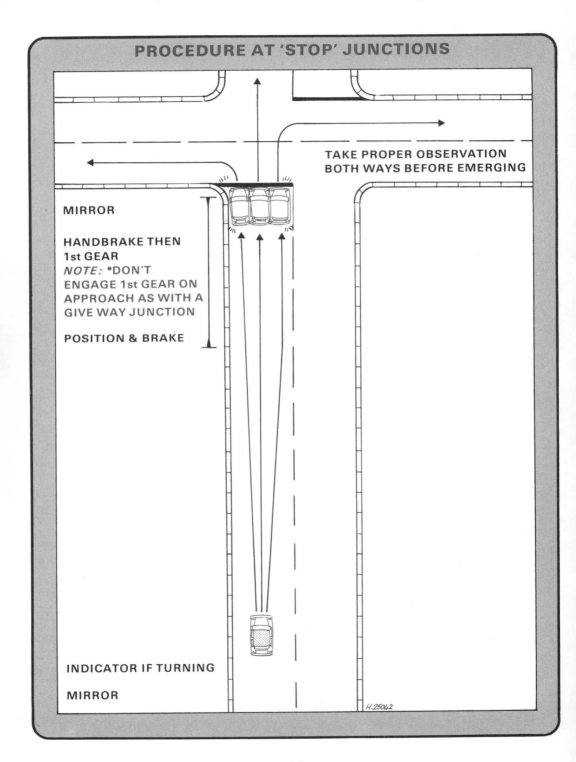

TAKE PROPER OBSERVATION
BOTH WAYS BEFORE EMERGING

MIRROR

HANDBRAKE THEN
1st GEAR
NOTE: *DON'T
ENGAGE 1st GEAR ON
APPROACH AS WITH A
GIVE WAY JUNCTION

POSITION & BRAKE

INDICATOR IF TURNING

MIRROR

H.25042

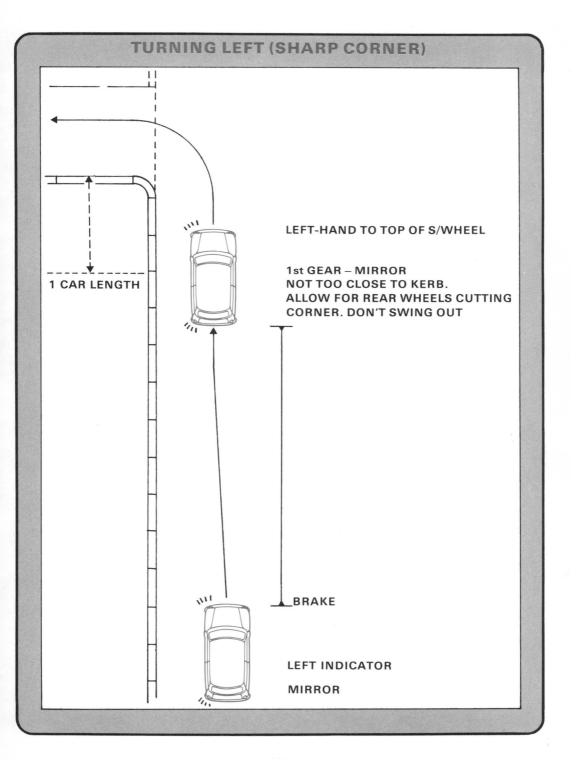

TURNING LEFT (SHARP CORNER)

1 CAR LENGTH

LEFT-HAND TO TOP OF S/WHEEL

1st GEAR – MIRROR
NOT TOO CLOSE TO KERB.
ALLOW FOR REAR WHEELS CUTTING
CORNER. DON'T SWING OUT

BRAKE

LEFT INDICATOR

MIRROR

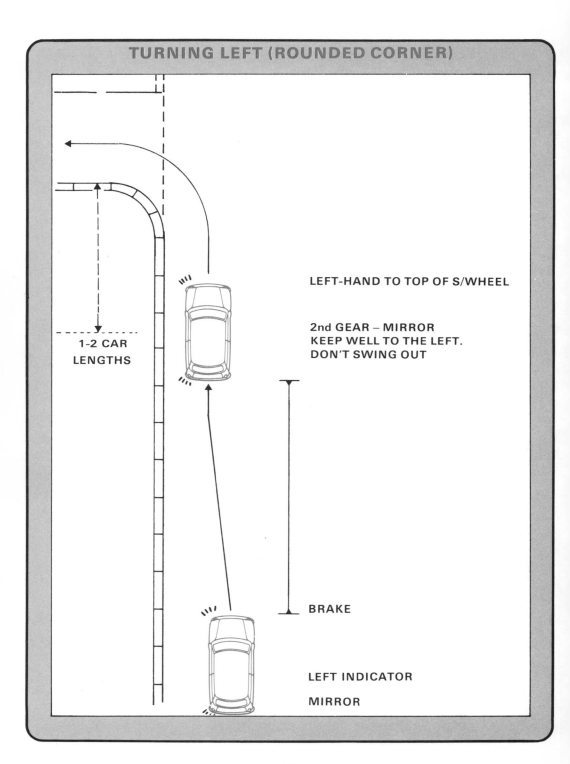

TURNING LEFT (ROUNDED CORNER)

1-2 CAR
LENGTHS

LEFT-HAND TO TOP OF S/WHEEL

2nd GEAR – MIRROR
KEEP WELL TO THE LEFT.
DON'T SWING OUT

BRAKE

LEFT INDICATOR

MIRROR

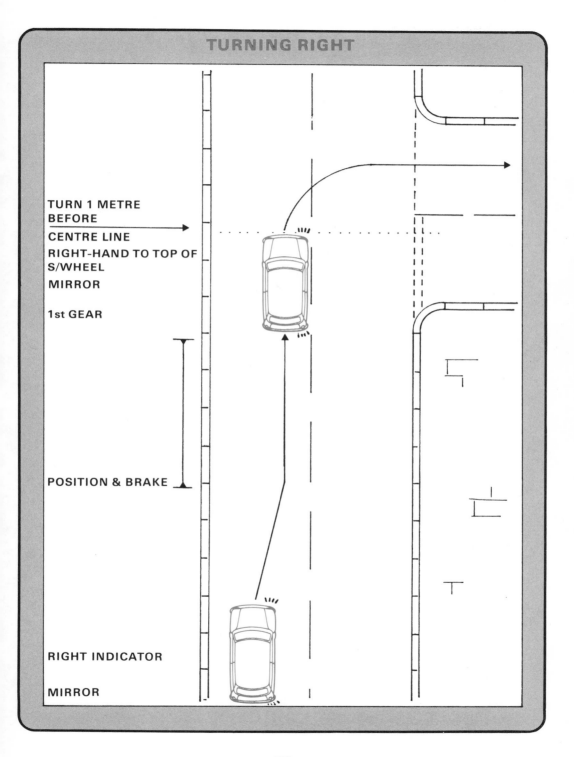

TURN 1 METRE
BEFORE

CENTRE LINE

RIGHT-HAND TO TOP OF
S/WHEEL

MIRROR

1st GEAR

POSITION & BRAKE

RIGHT INDICATOR

MIRROR

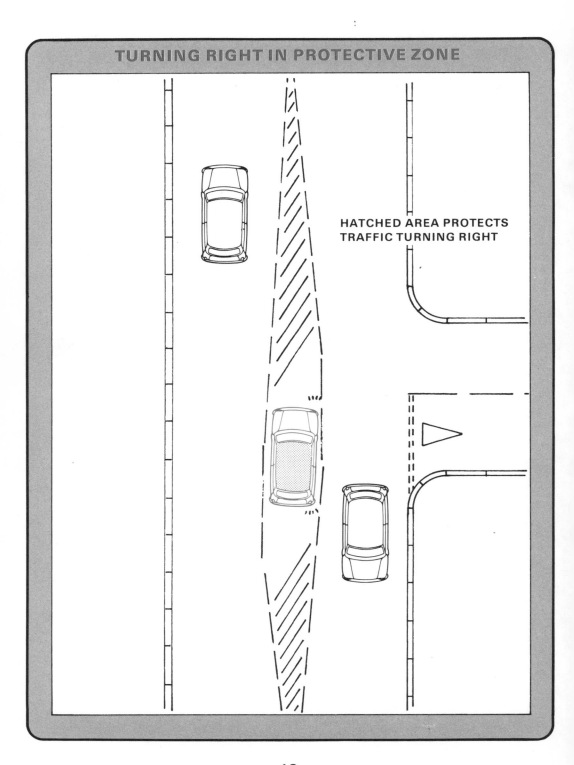

HATCHED AREA PROTECTS
TRAFFIC TURNING RIGHT

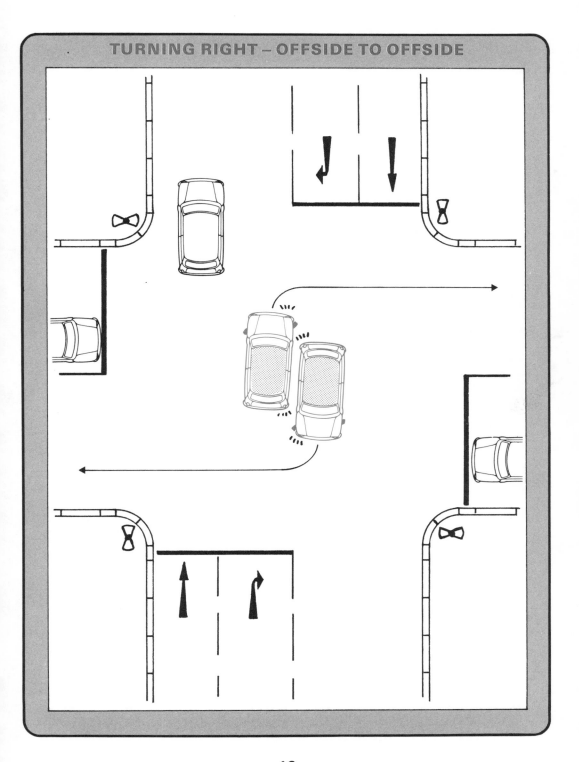

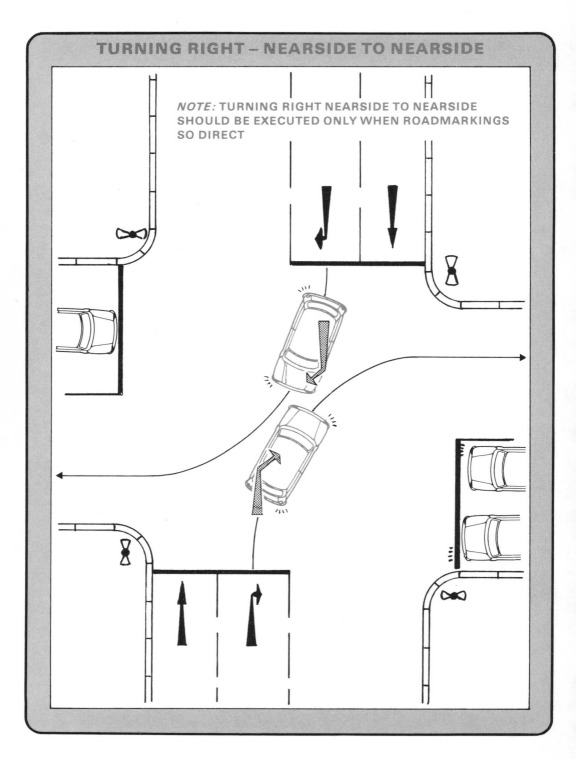

USE OF A BOX JUNCTION

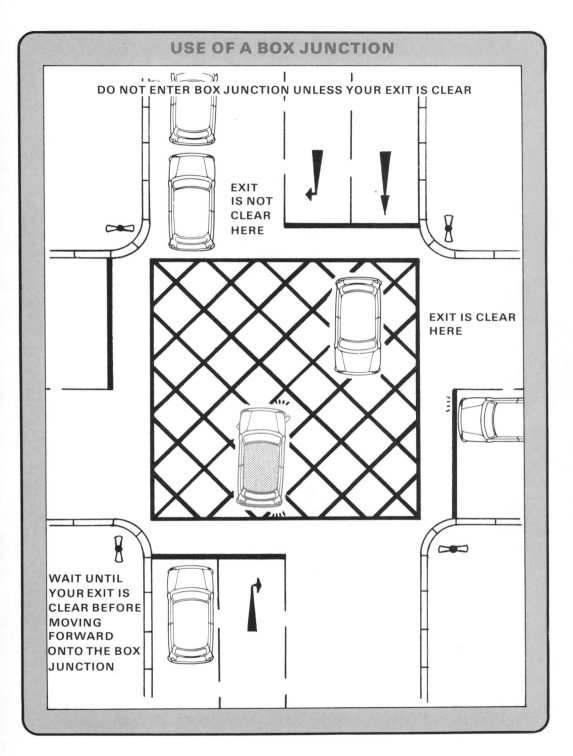

DO NOT ENTER BOX JUNCTION UNLESS YOUR EXIT IS CLEAR

EXIT
IS NOT
CLEAR
HERE

EXIT IS CLEAR
HERE

WAIT UNTIL
YOUR EXIT IS
CLEAR BEFORE
MOVING
FORWARD
ONTO THE BOX
JUNCTION

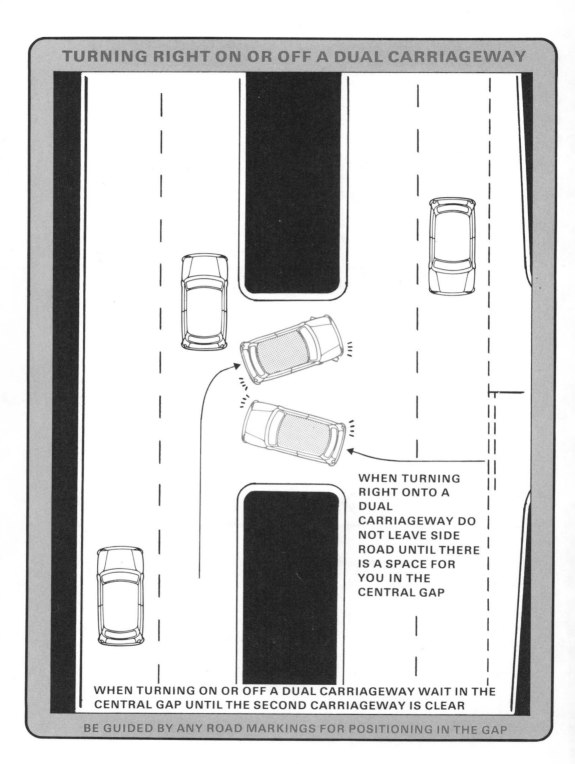

TURNING RIGHT ON OR OFF A DUAL CARRIAGEWAY

WHEN TURNING RIGHT ONTO A DUAL CARRIAGEWAY DO NOT LEAVE SIDE ROAD UNTIL THERE IS A SPACE FOR YOU IN THE CENTRAL GAP

WHEN TURNING ON OR OFF A DUAL CARRIAGEWAY WAIT IN THE CENTRAL GAP UNTIL THE SECOND CARRIAGEWAY IS CLEAR

BE GUIDED BY ANY ROAD MARKINGS FOR POSITIONING IN THE GAP

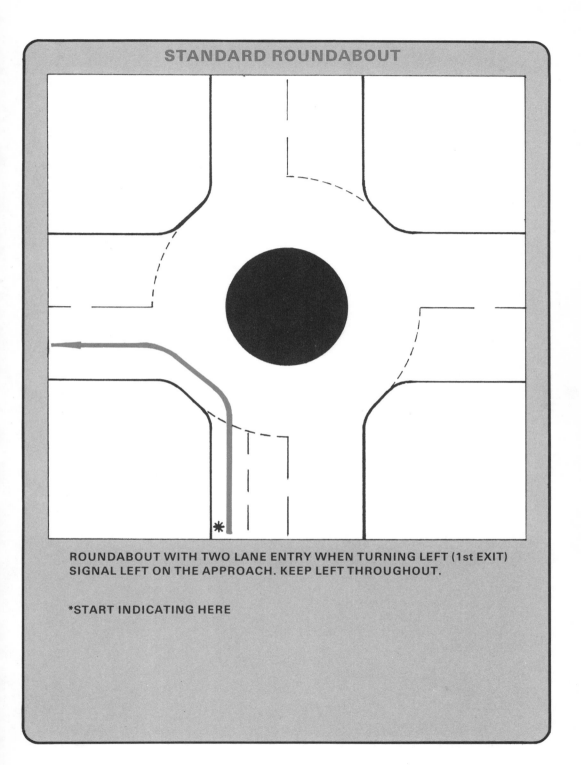

ROUNDABOUT WITH TWO LANE ENTRY WHEN TURNING LEFT (1st EXIT)
SIGNAL LEFT ON THE APPROACH. KEEP LEFT THROUGHOUT.

*START INDICATING HERE

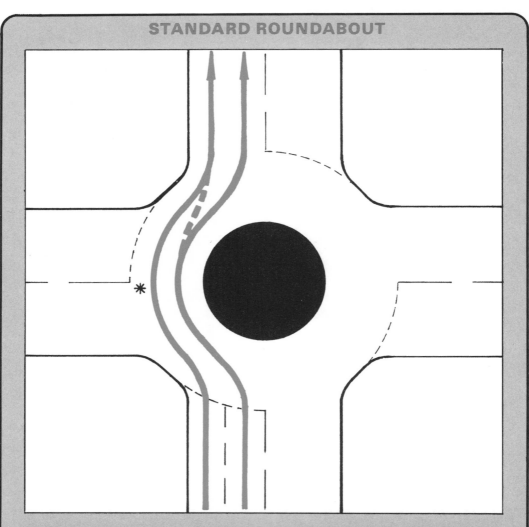

ROUNDABOUT WITH TWO LANE ENTRY WHEN GOING STRAIGHT AHEAD (2nd EXIT)
APPROACH IN THE LEFT HAND LANE. KEEP TO THAT LANE ON THE ROUNDABOUT. LEAVE ON THE LEFT.
IF CONDITIONS PREVENT THIS THE ALTERNATIVE ROUTE MAY BE USED, ie. THE LANE IS BLOCKED OR YOU INTEND TO TURN RIGHT SHORTLY AFTER LEAVING THE ROUNDABOUT

*START INDICATING HERE

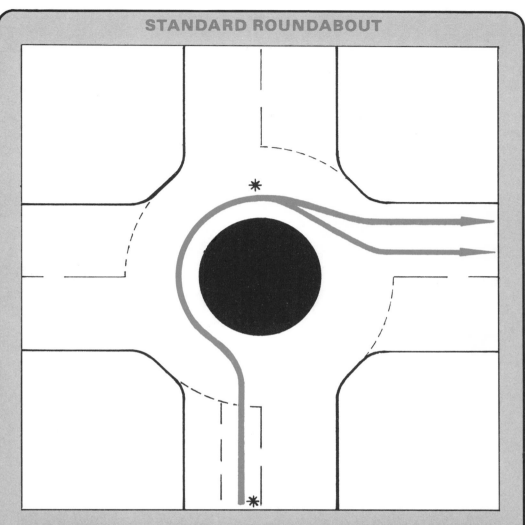

ROUNDABOUT WITH TWO LANE ENTRY WHEN TURNING RIGHT (3rd EXIT) APPROACH IN THE RIGHT-HAND LANE. USE THE RIGHT INDICATOR BEFORE ENTERING AND KEEP IN THE RIGHT-HAND LANE. CHANGE TO THE LEFT INDICATOR AT THE EXIT BEFORE THE ONE YOU INTEND LEAVING BY

*START INDICATING HERE

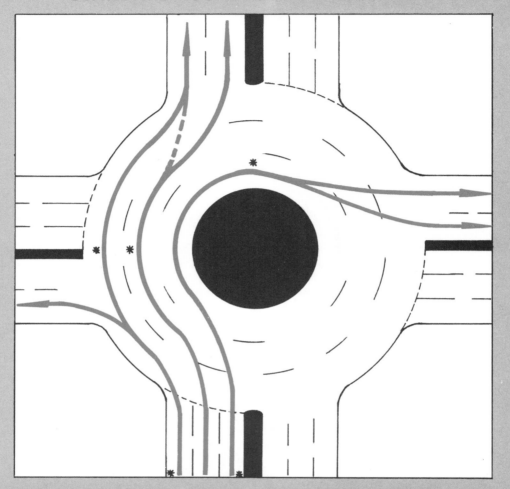

USE THE L.H. LANE FOR TURNING LEFT (1st EXIT). SIGNAL LEFT ON APPROACH
USE THE L.H. OR THE CENTRE LANE FOR GOING STRAIGHT AHEAD (2nd EXIT)
USE THE R.H. LANE WHEN TURNING RIGHT (3rd EXIT). SIGNAL RIGHT ON APPROACH

IN EACH CASE SIGNAL LEFT AT THE EXIT BEFORE THE ONE YOU INTEND LEAVING BY. CHECK YOUR MIRROR AND OVER YOUR LEFT SHOULDER BEFORE DOING SO.

WHICHEVER LANE YOU SELECT ON APPROACH, KEEP TO THAT LANE THROUGHOUT UNTIL YOU SIGNAL TO LEAVE
USE THE MOST LEFT OF ANY OPTIONS AVAILABLE AND BE GUIDED BY ROAD MARKINGS OR SIGNS

*START INDICATING HERE

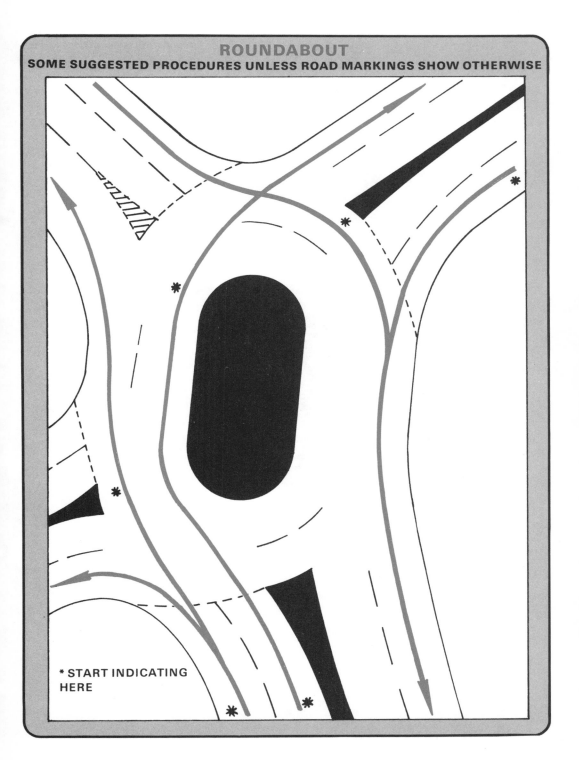

ROUNDABOUT
SOME SUGGESTED PROCEDURES UNLESS ROAD MARKINGS SHOW OTHERWISE

* START INDICATING
HERE

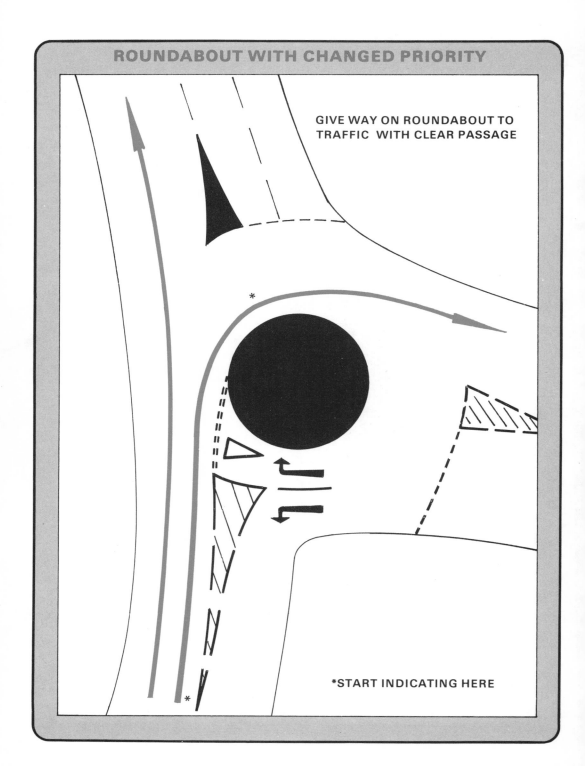

GIVE WAY ON ROUNDABOUT TO TRAFFIC WITH CLEAR PASSAGE

*START INDICATING HERE

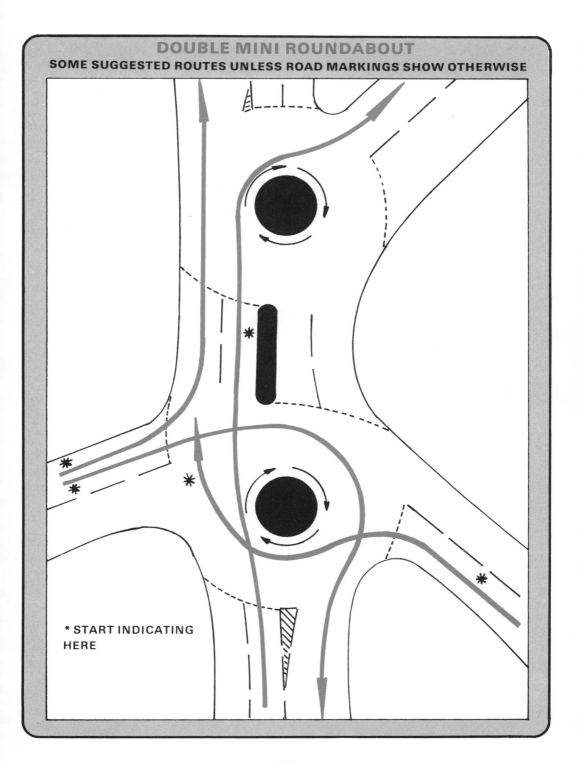

DOUBLE MINI ROUNDABOUT
SOME SUGGESTED ROUTES UNLESS ROAD MARKINGS SHOW OTHERWISE

* START INDICATING
HERE

MULTI-ROUNDABOUT

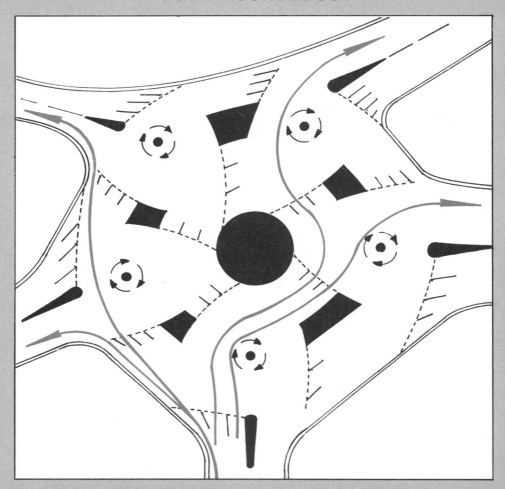

A VARIETY OF OPTIONS ARE AVAILABLE ON THIS TYPE OF ROUNDABOUT. GENERALLY ACCEPTABLE ROUTES ARE SHOWN. FOR THE 1st TWO EXITS KEEP LEFT & NEGOTIATE CLOCKWISE. FOR THE 3rd 4th & 5th APPROACH ON THE RIGHT, NEGOTIATE THE CENTRAL ISLAND ANTICLOCKWISE AND THEN NEGOTIATE THE MINI ROUNDABOUTS CLOCKWISE. SIGNALS HAVE BEEN OMITTED FROM THE DIAGRAM TO AVOID CONFUSION AS THEY COULD VARY SOMEWHAT BETWEEN ROUNDABOUTS OF A SIMILAR NATURE

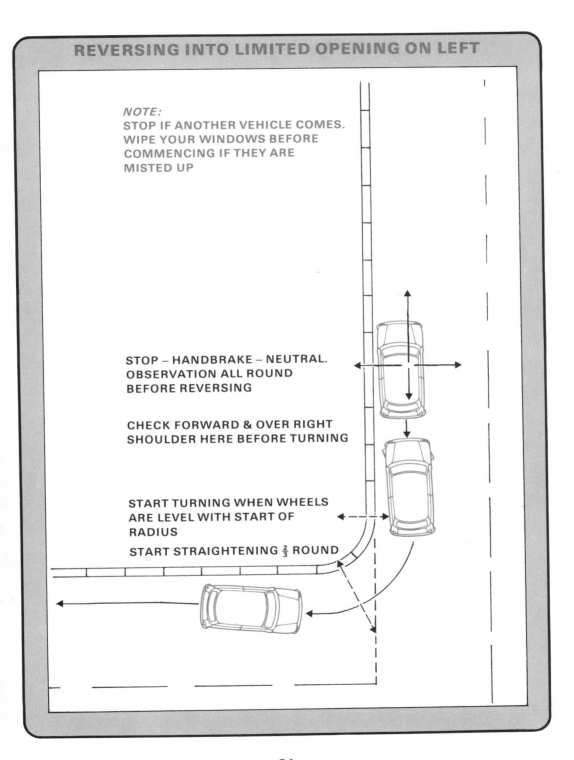

NOTE:
STOP IF ANOTHER VEHICLE COMES.
WIPE YOUR WINDOWS BEFORE
COMMENCING IF THEY ARE
MISTED UP

STOP – HANDBRAKE – NEUTRAL.
OBSERVATION ALL ROUND
BEFORE REVERSING

CHECK FORWARD & OVER RIGHT
SHOULDER HERE BEFORE TURNING

START TURNING WHEN WHEELS
ARE LEVEL WITH START OF
RADIUS

START STRAIGHTENING $\frac{2}{3}$ ROUND

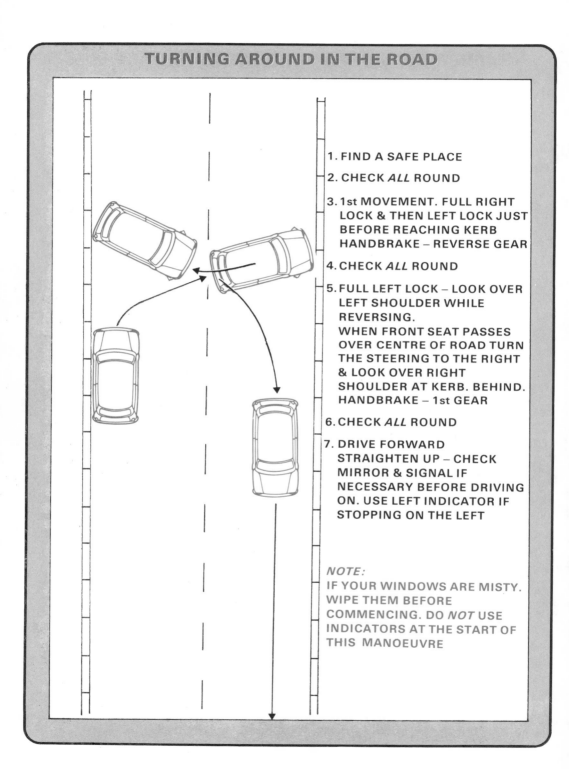

TURNING AROUND IN THE ROAD

1. FIND A SAFE PLACE

2. CHECK *ALL* ROUND

3. 1st MOVEMENT. FULL RIGHT LOCK & THEN LEFT LOCK JUST BEFORE REACHING KERB HANDBRAKE – REVERSE GEAR

4. CHECK *ALL* ROUND

5. FULL LEFT LOCK – LOOK OVER LEFT SHOULDER WHILE REVERSING. WHEN FRONT SEAT PASSES OVER CENTRE OF ROAD TURN THE STEERING TO THE RIGHT & LOOK OVER RIGHT SHOULDER AT KERB. BEHIND. HANDBRAKE – 1st GEAR

6. CHECK *ALL* ROUND

7. DRIVE FORWARD STRAIGHTEN UP – CHECK MIRROR & SIGNAL IF NECESSARY BEFORE DRIVING ON. USE LEFT INDICATOR IF STOPPING ON THE LEFT

NOTE:
IF YOUR WINDOWS ARE MISTY. WIPE THEM BEFORE COMMENCING. DO *NOT* USE INDICATORS AT THE START OF THIS MANOEUVRE

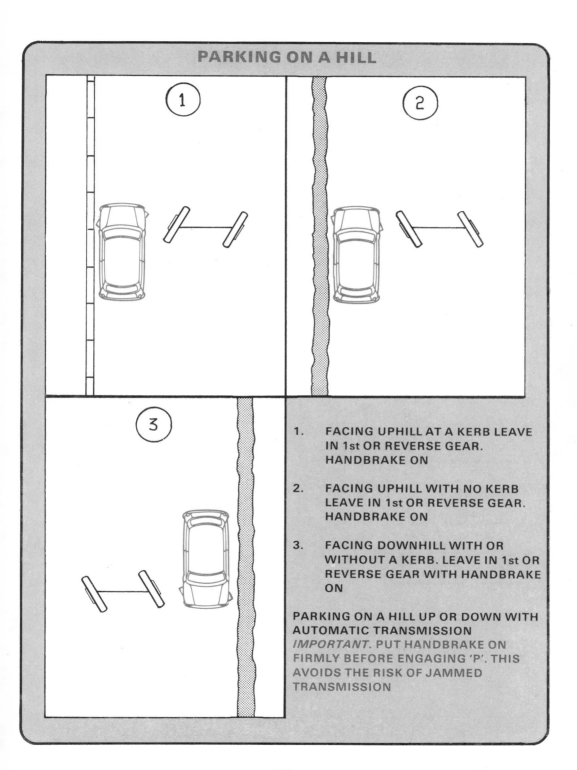

PARKING ON A HILL

1. **FACING UPHILL AT A KERB LEAVE IN 1st OR REVERSE GEAR. HANDBRAKE ON**

2. **FACING UPHILL WITH NO KERB LEAVE IN 1st OR REVERSE GEAR. HANDBRAKE ON**

3. **FACING DOWNHILL WITH OR WITHOUT A KERB. LEAVE IN 1st OR REVERSE GEAR WITH HANDBRAKE ON**

PARKING ON A HILL UP OR DOWN WITH AUTOMATIC TRANSMISSION
IMPORTANT. PUT HANDBRAKE ON FIRMLY BEFORE ENGAGING 'P'. THIS AVOIDS THE RISK OF JAMMED TRANSMISSION

PARKING IN A CAR PARK

IT IS GENERALLY ADVISABLE TO REVERSE YOUR CAR INTO A PARKING SPACE. THIS ENABLES YOU TO PARK MORE SQUARELY AND MEANS YOU DRIVE FORWARD WHEN LEAVING

$\frac{2}{3}$ TO LEFT $\frac{2}{3}$ TO RIGHT

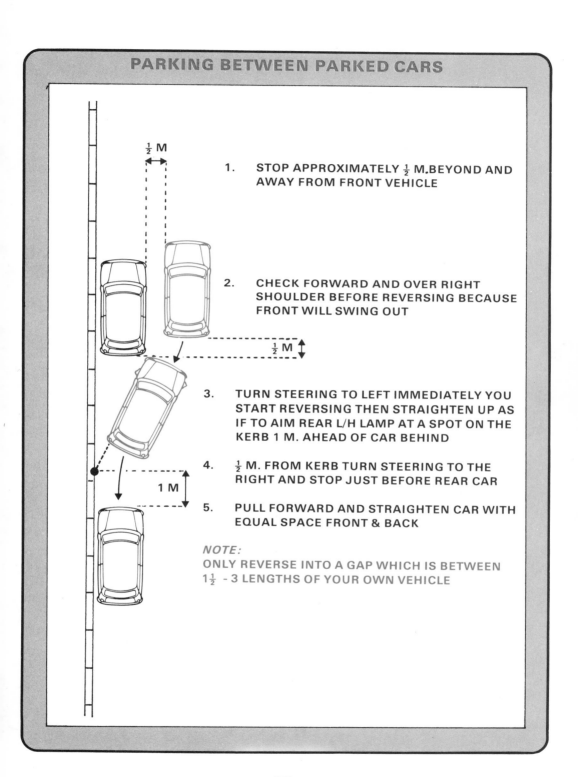

$\frac{1}{2}$ M

1. STOP APPROXIMATELY $\frac{1}{2}$ M. BEYOND AND AWAY FROM FRONT VEHICLE

2. CHECK FORWARD AND OVER RIGHT SHOULDER BEFORE REVERSING BECAUSE FRONT WILL SWING OUT

$\frac{1}{2}$ M

3. TURN STEERING TO LEFT IMMEDIATELY YOU START REVERSING THEN STRAIGHTEN UP AS IF TO AIM REAR L/H LAMP AT A SPOT ON THE KERB 1 M. AHEAD OF CAR BEHIND

4. $\frac{1}{2}$ M. FROM KERB TURN STEERING TO THE RIGHT AND STOP JUST BEFORE REAR CAR

1 M

5. PULL FORWARD AND STRAIGHTEN CAR WITH EQUAL SPACE FRONT & BACK

NOTE:
ONLY REVERSE INTO A GAP WHICH IS BETWEEN $1\frac{1}{2}$ - 3 LENGTHS OF YOUR OWN VEHICLE

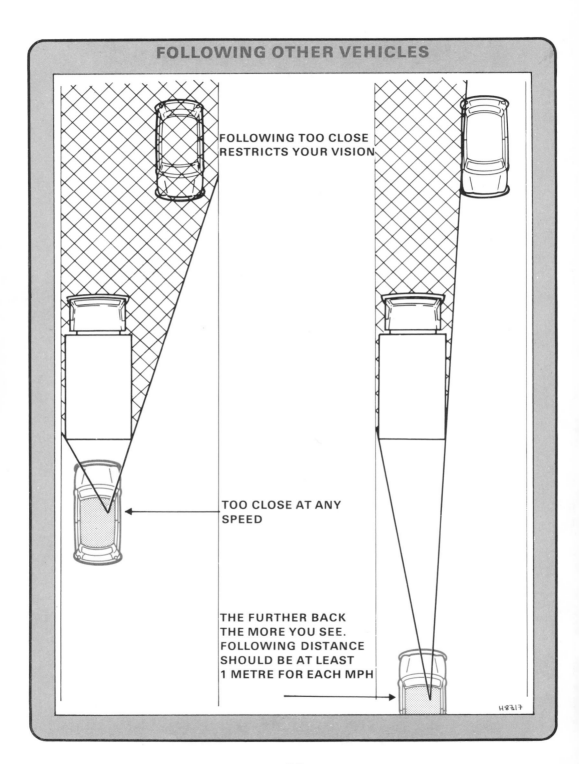

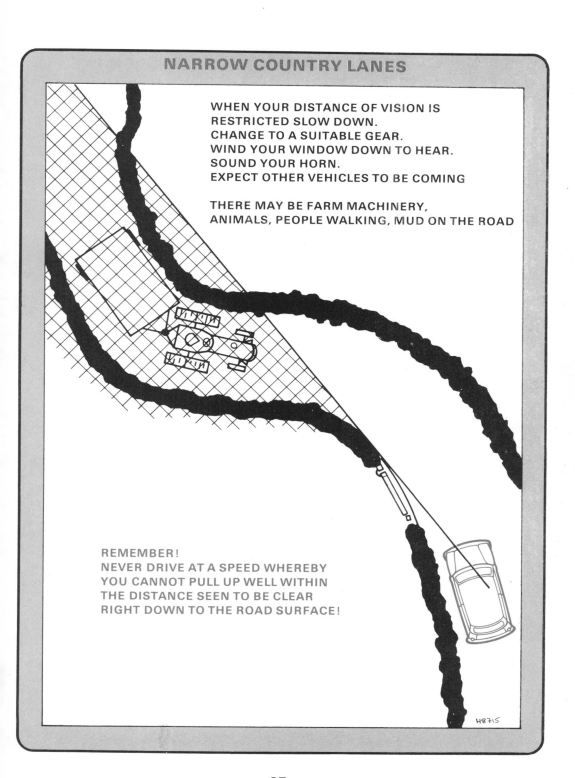

WHEN YOUR DISTANCE OF VISION IS
RESTRICTED SLOW DOWN.
CHANGE TO A SUITABLE GEAR.
WIND YOUR WINDOW DOWN TO HEAR.
SOUND YOUR HORN.
EXPECT OTHER VEHICLES TO BE COMING

THERE MAY BE FARM MACHINERY,
ANIMALS, PEOPLE WALKING, MUD ON THE ROAD

REMEMBER!
NEVER DRIVE AT A SPEED WHEREBY
YOU CANNOT PULL UP WELL WITHIN
THE DISTANCE SEEN TO BE CLEAR
RIGHT DOWN TO THE ROAD SURFACE!

H8715

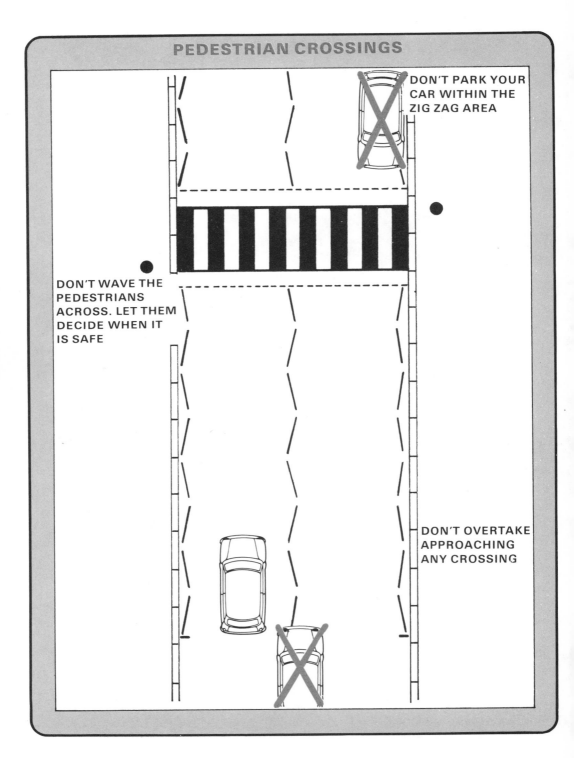

DON'T PARK YOUR CAR WITHIN THE ZIG ZAG AREA

DON'T WAVE THE PEDESTRIANS ACROSS. LET THEM DECIDE WHEN IT IS SAFE

DON'T OVERTAKE APPROACHING ANY CROSSING

SOME POINTS TO CONSIDER BEFORE
OVERTAKING:

1. SPEED AND LENGTH OF VEHICLE
   TO BE OVERTAKEN
2. LENGTH OF ROAD AHEAD SEEN
   TO BE CLEAR
3. FOLLOWING TRAFFIC
4. ROAD SURFACE CONDITION
5. SIDE TURNINGS, EMERGING
   VEHICLES
6. THE CAPABILITIES OF YOUR
   VEHICLE

**OVERTAKING IS THE
MOST HAZARDOUS
DRIVING MANOEUVRE**
*IF IN DOUBT DON'T
OVERTAKE AT ALL!*

DON'T CUT IN TOO
SOON

ALLOW PLENTY OF
ROOM

SOUND HORN IF
NECESSARY

POSITION CAR
FOR BEST VIEW
AHEAD;

IF SAFE TO OVERTAKE:
a) CHECK MIRRORS
   AND SIGNAL IF
   NECESSARY
b) SELECT MOST
   SUITABLE GEAR
   FOR BEST
   ACCELERATION
c) CHECK ALL IS
   CLEAR BEHIND
   BEFORE MOVING
   OUT

H.25041

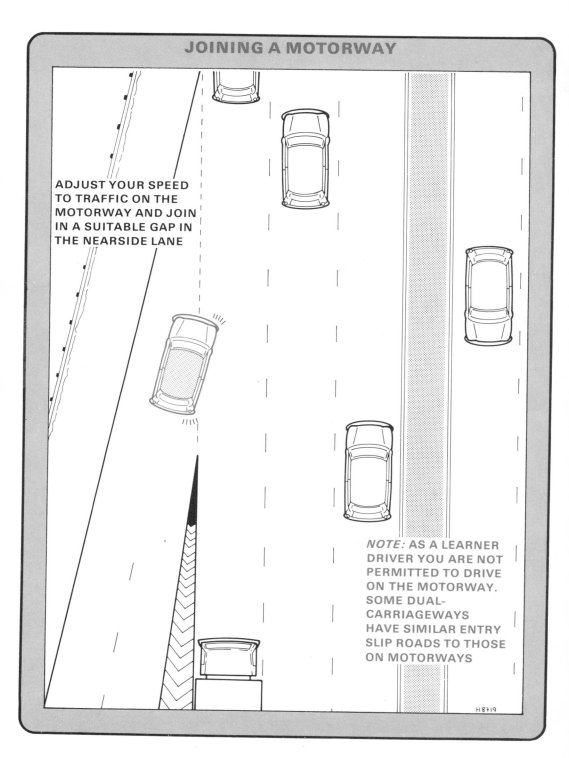

ADJUST YOUR SPEED TO TRAFFIC ON THE MOTORWAY AND JOIN IN A SUITABLE GAP IN THE NEARSIDE LANE

NOTE: AS A LEARNER DRIVER YOU ARE NOT PERMITTED TO DRIVE ON THE MOTORWAY. SOME DUAL-CARRIAGEWAYS HAVE SIMILAR ENTRY SLIP ROADS TO THOSE ON MOTORWAYS

H8719

DAILY CHECKS

It is your responsibility to ensure that your vehicle is safe in all respects. Although you may not be mechanically-minded it is possible for you to carry out certain basic checks on your vehicle at regular intervals.

Your instructor should show you how to do the following:

Check the oil level.

Check the water in the radiator.

Check the brake and clutch fluid.

Check the level in the battery.

Check the washer bottle.

How to inflate the tyres and check them over.

How to change a wheel.

How to fill up with petrol.

SOME ADVICE CONCERNING YOUR TEST

The most important thing is that you are ready for it. Don't try your luck if you feel you need more time; postpone it for a few weeks giving yourself more time to practise.

It is essential to get a good night's sleep before the big day; there is nothing worse than a fuzzy head which will prevent you from thinking clearly and positively whilst on the test.

There is no truth whatsoever in the old tale that the examiner 'never passes anyone on Thursday afternoon', or that they only pass so many each day. Their job is to ensure that the candidate is competent to drive without danger to, and with due consideration for, other users of the road. That is all they are concerned with so whatever sex, age or nationality you are makes no difference at all.

The examiner is aware that you probably feel a little nervous but you will find that you soon settle down and feel at ease.

You should arrive at the test centre at least 15 minutes early giving you time to relax a little before the test begins. Ensure that you leave your vehicle in a safe place nearby and that you conform to any waiting regulations which may be in force.

Make sure your vehicle is reasonably tidy and clean, and the safety straps are properly functional. The examiner will not want to spend time untangling a dirty twisted belt.

Have all the windows open about $\frac{1}{2}$ inch. This will help to prevent misting up especially is it is raining. Should your windows mist up at any time it will be your duty to wipe them clean, but find a safe place to stop and do this.

Before you even get into your vehicle you will have to read a number plate of $3\frac{1}{2}$ inch letters from a distance of 75 feet, and 67 feet if the letters are $3\frac{1}{8}$" high. If your eyesight does not meet these requirements then you will fail the test at once. The use of spectacles is, however, permitted.

Should you make any mistakes, such as 'clip' the kerb or stall the engine, do not assume that this will fail you and therefore give up. Take a deep breath and carry on. The examiner will decide whether or not any mistakes are sufficient to fail you at the end of the test.

Make sure you know your *Highway Code* thoroughly as it is not unknown for a candidate to give an exceptionally good drive and then fail because of not being able to answer a simple question from the Highway Code.

SOME COMMON REASONS FOR FAILURE OF THE TEST

Forgetting to look over your shoulder before moving off.

Not putting wipers on if it is raining, before moving off at the start of the test.

Co-ordination of clutch and throttle pedal.

Approaching hazards or junctions too fast.

Swinging out before turning left.

Driving over the centre of the road after turning left.

Bad positioning before turning right.

Putting the clutch down too late when stopping or slowing.

Insufficient or late use of the mirror.

Passing too close to parked vehicles.

Failure to take proper observation both ways before emerging at a junction.

Not completely stopping at 'STOP' sign. (The reason for insistence on use of handbrake.)

Reversing around a corner without being under control.

Driving too slowly or too fast.

Misjudging the speed of traffic from the right on roundabouts.

Not looking over the left shoulder before crossing the lane when leaving roundabouts.

Insufficient observation before manoeuvring.

Not studying the *Highway Code* and roadsigns.

Remember, the more practice and good instruction you have the more likely you are to pass the first time.